What Is Hearing?

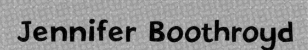

Jennifer Boothroyd

Lerner Publications Company
Minneapolis

Lerner Publications Company
A division of Lerner Publishing Group, Inc.
241 First Avenue North
Minneapolis, MN 55401 U.S.A.

Website address: www.lernerbooks.com

Library of Congress Cataloging-in-Publication Data

Boothroyd, Jennifer, 1972–
    What is hearing? / by Jennifer Boothroyd.
        p.   cm. — (Lightning bolt books™—Your amazing senses)
    Includes index.
    ISBN 978–0–7613–4250–2 (lib. bdg. : alk. paper)
        1. Hearing—Juvenile literature. I. Title.
    QP462.2.B66 2010
    612.8´5—dc22   2008051848

Manufactured in the United States of America
1 2 3 4 5 6 — BP — 15 14 13 12 11 10

Contents

Gathering Information

Listen! What noises do you hear around you?

Do you
hear the
soft ticking
of a watch?
Or the steady tap
of rain against
your window?

The gentle patter
of a springtime
shower is one of
many sounds that
fill our world.

5

Hearing is one of your five senses.

You use your ears to hear things.

Your ears pick up a lot of sounds, from blaring sirens to quiet whispers.

Your sense of hearing helps you learn about the world.

It can also protect you from danger.

Your Ears

How do your ears help you hear? **Sound travels through the air in waves.**

Sound waves carry noises to your ears.

The waves hit your eardrum. Your eardrum vibrates. This causes three tiny bones inside your ear to move.

A tuning fork makes a musical tone that sets off vibrations in your ear.

The bones send a message through a tube called the cochlea. Then the message travels through nerves into your brain.

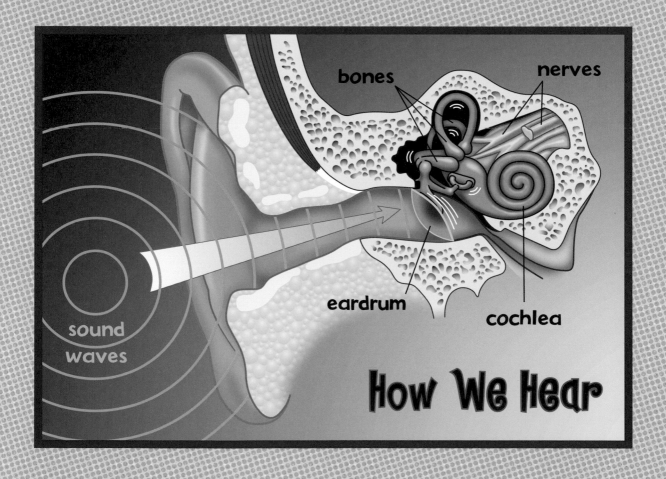

bones

nerves

eardrum

cochlea

sound waves

How We Hear

Volume

Your ears can hear sounds at different volumes.

Volume has to do with how loud a sound is. When you turn music up or down, you're adjusting the volume.

Some sounds are quiet—
like rustling leaves.

Or a crackling campfire.

Campfire logs pop and snap as they burn.

Some sounds
are loud—like
exploding
fireworks.

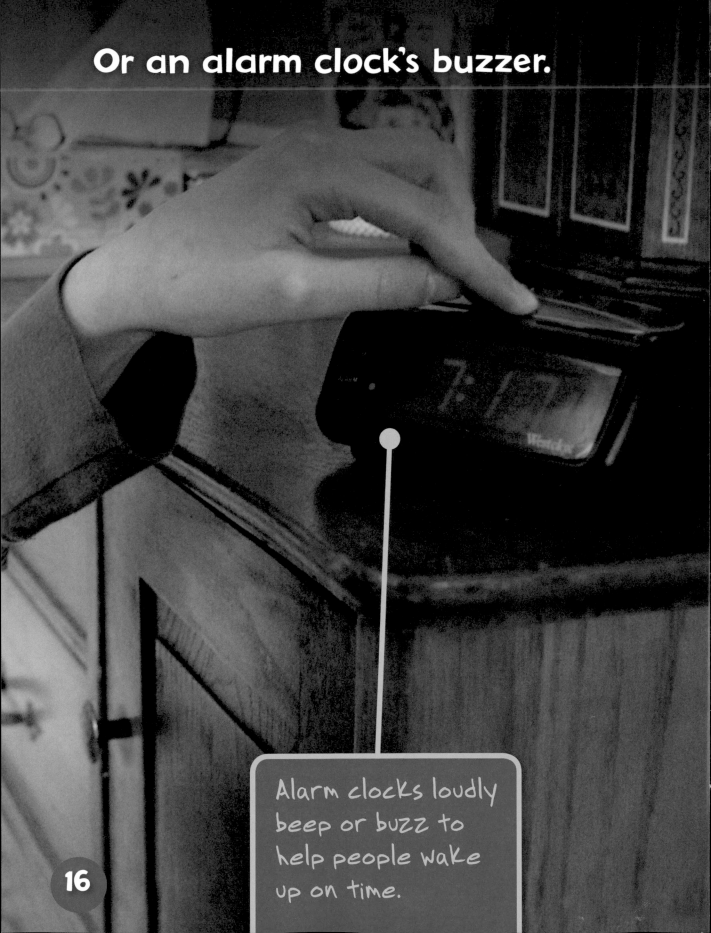

Or an alarm clock's buzzer.

Alarm clocks loudly beep or buzz to help people wake up on time.

Pitch

Your ears can hear sounds at different pitches. Some sounds are high—like the tinkling of chimes.

Or the squeak of a swing.

High sounds are produced when sound waves move quickly.

Other sounds are low—like
a cat's rumbling purr.

Or a bass drum's low thud.

Low sounds are produced when sound waves move slowly.

Protection from Danger

Our hearing protects us from danger.

Your ears and eyes both help you know when it is safe to cross the street.

We freeze when someone yells, "Stop!"

A fire alarm tells us to get out of the building.

Fire alarms use sound to alert us to danger.

Hearing and Your Feelings

Sounds can change the way you feel. A song may make you feel sad.

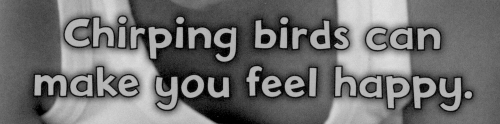

Chirping birds can make you feel happy.

Emotions and sounds are closely connected. What sounds make you happy?

25

Someone's scream may annoy you.

Hearing is an important sense. You use it every day.

Hearing lets us use speech to communicate with friends.

27

Activity

Who Is Speaking?

Ask an adult if you can try this experiment to test your sense of hearing.

What you need:

a group of at least six friends

What you do:

Have everyone in the group sit in a circle. Choose one person to be the listener and another to be the leader. The listener lies down in the center of the circle and closes his or her eyes.

The leader silently chooses one person to be the speaker. The speaker says hello to the listener. The listener needs to identify the speaker. Too easy? Have the speaker disguise his or her voice. Need more of a challenge? Have two speakers say hello at the same time. See if the listener can identify both of the speakers. If you really want to test yourself, try turning on the TV or the radio or having the people in the circle sing a song such as *Row, Row, Row Your Boat* while the speaker says hello.

Glossary

cochlea: a tube in the ear that allows us to hear

eardrum: a membrane inside the ear that vibrates when sound strikes it

nerve: one of the thin fibers that sends messages between your brain and other parts of your body

pitch: the highness or lowness of a sound

sense: one of the powers that people and animals use to learn about their surroundings. The five senses are sight, hearing, touch, taste, and smell.

vibrate: to quickly move back and forth

volume: loudness

wave: a vibration of energy that travels through air or water

Further Reading

BBC Schools Science Clips: Sound and Hearing
http://www.bbc.co.uk/schools/scienceclips/
ages/5_6/sound_hearing.shtml

Hewitt, Sally. *Hear This!* New York: Crabtree, 2008.

KidsHealth: How the Body Works
http://kidshealth.org/kid/htbw

Nelson, Robin. *Seeing and Hearing Well.* Minneapolis: Lerner Publications Company, 2006.

Rotner, Shelley. *Senses in the City.* Minneapolis: Millbrook Press, 2008.

Rotner, Shelley. *Senses on the Farm.* Minneapolis: Millbrook Press, 2009.

Index

Photo Acknowledgments

The images in this book are used with the permission of: © alphababy/Dreamstime.com, p. 1; © iStockphoto.com/Donna Coleman, p. 2; © iStockphoto.com/Jaren Wicklund, p. 4; © iStockphoto.com/Steve Stone, p. 5; © Jamie Grill/Iconica/Getty Images, p. 6; © iStockphoto.com/Pathathai Chungyam, p. 7; © Gary John Norman/Taxi/Getty Images, p. 8; © Meg Takamura/IZA Stock/Getty Images, p. 9; © Robert Llewellyn/Imagestate/Photolibrary, p. 10; © Laura Westlund/Independent Picture Service, p. 11; © iStockphoto.com/Jaimie Duplass, p. 12; © Dana Tezarr/Photonica/Getty Images, p. 13; © iStockphoto.com/Nicole S. Young, p. 14; © Hiroshi Watanabe/Taxi Japan/Getty Images, p. 15; © Julie Caruso, p. 16; © iStockphoto.com/blaneyphoto, p. 17; © Christopher Robbins/Digital Vision/Getty Images, p. 18; © Ligia Botero/The Image Bank/Getty Images, p. 19; © ThinkStock/SuperStock, p. 20; Custom Medical Stock Photo , p. 21; © charmayne carava/Alamy, p. 22; © Jeff Greenberg/The Image Works, p. 23; Reflexstock, p. 24; © Image Source/Getty Images, pp. 25, 27; © age fotostock/SuperStock, p. 26; © Tay Rees/Riser/Getty Images, p. 29; © Hill Street Studios/Blend Images/Getty Images, p. 30; © iStockphoto.com/Doug Schneider, p. 31.

Front cover: © Firststar/Dreamstime.com.